THE SPECTACLE
Celebrating the History of the Indianapolis 500

WRITTEN & ILLUSTRATED BY CHRIS WORKMAN
FOREWORD BY RYAN HUNTER-REAY

FOR THE THOUSANDS of drivers, crew members, engineers, manufacturers and other devoted men & women who have competed in, and helped organize and run, the Indy 500.

IN HONOR OF MY MOM, whose never-ending support pushed me to chase my dream of creating children's books about racing. Her sudden diagnosis of and passing from cancer sparked my desire to help find a cure.

IN SUPPORT OF the millions of children & adults who have fought this elusive disease.

"The Spectacle - Celebrating the History of the Indianapolis 500" is proudly printed in the USA for domestic consumption. International vendors may be used for production in other markets.

First printing January 2017. ISBN: 978-0996286954

Published by Apex Legends, a division of Apex Communications Group, LLC.

ACKNOWLEDGEMENTS

Special thanks to AJ Foyt Racing, Andretti Autosport, Team Penske, Chip Ganassi Racing, the Indianapolis Motor Speedway and the Verizon IndyCar Series staff for your help & support in bringing this project to life, and to Indianapolis Motor Speedway Hall of Fame Historian Donald Davidson for reviewing and fact-checking my work. And, thank you to the motorsports media who have helped spread the word about this project. Lastly, a note of appreciation to Racing for Cancer director Tom Vossman and Ryan Hunter-Reay for their partnership.

To Brian Bonner, Tom Moore and Rob Howden - thank you for your help and guidance through this process. Most importantly, thanks to my wife and kids for your ongoing patience and support!

FROM THE AUTHOR

Creating "The Spectacle - Celebrating the History of the Indianapolis 500" has been nothing short of an amazing process!

As an avid open-wheel racing fan, the opportunity to learn about this wonderful event and interact with a number of teams, Indianapolis Motor Speedway Historian Donald Davidson and the Verizon IndyCar Series team was a rewarding experience.

As you may imagine, it has been a challenge to take 100 races worth of amazing content and fit it all into a children's book that is engaging for kids.

Not every driver, team and car could be included; sadly I had to cut sections to prevent the book from getting any longer. Hopefully, you understand if any personal favorites were omitted.

I hope this book not only helps you learn about "The Greatest Spectacle in Racing," but that it inspires you, whether you are five-years-old or fifty, to fall in love with the sights, sounds, action and drama that have made the Indy 500 a hallmark American event for over a century.

- Chris Workman

NAVIGATING THE BOOK:

The history of the Indianapolis 500 is divided into a series of short sections. While the book loosely follows a chronological flow, readers can jump into any of these book sections at any time.

Please note: it is not necessary to read the text cover-to-cover... although you'll get a true sense of how the "Greatest Spectacle in Racing" has evolved over the years if you do!

CONTENTS

FOREWORD
RYAN HUNTER-REAY, 2014 INDY 500-WINNER

It is not often in my profession that I am presented an opportunity to help promote a book, much less a children's book! In fact, only four short years ago, it probably wouldn't have even crossed my mind.

But today, as a father of three beautiful boys, having personally met so many children who have been affected by cancer, I know firsthand how important it is to connect with children to share our dreams, our passion, and our stories to help them create their own.

Chris has done a great job in this book connecting with children by describing racing in a way all of us can understand while possibly igniting a "spark" of interest in a sport I've built my entire life around.

I recall when my father first shared his love for racing with me and I can only imagine how a book like this would have helped inspire me even more to fulfill my childhood dreams.

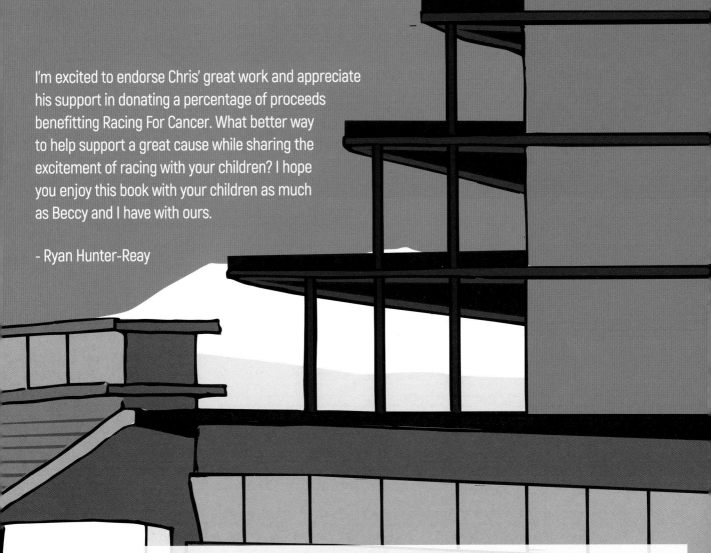

I'm excited to endorse Chris' great work and appreciate his support in donating a percentage of proceeds benefitting Racing For Cancer. What better way to help support a great cause while sharing the excitement of racing with your children? I hope you enjoy this book with your children as much as Beccy and I have with ours.

- Ryan Hunter-Reay

"HELPING PICK UP THE PACE... ONE FAN AT A TIME!

Ryan Hunter-Reay founded Racing For Cancer in 2010 following his mother's passing from cancer. Since then, Racing for Cancer has been focused on a goal of bringing motorsports fans, teams, drivers, and sponsors together to join in the fight to beat cancer.

Through various fundraising programs they provide support to help individuals, families, and children who are battling cancer. They focus their efforts towards early detection and prevention because nearly one third of all cancer is said to be preventable.

They use the sport of racing to increase awareness and to raise funds for new facilities. And, they conduct hospital visits to lift the spirits of sick children and their families.

Please visit racingforcancer.com for more information or to donate to their cause!

racing for cancer
HELPING PICK UP THE PACE

APEX LEGENDS IS A PROUD SPONSOR OF RACING FOR CANCER

"WHAT IS THIS THING?"

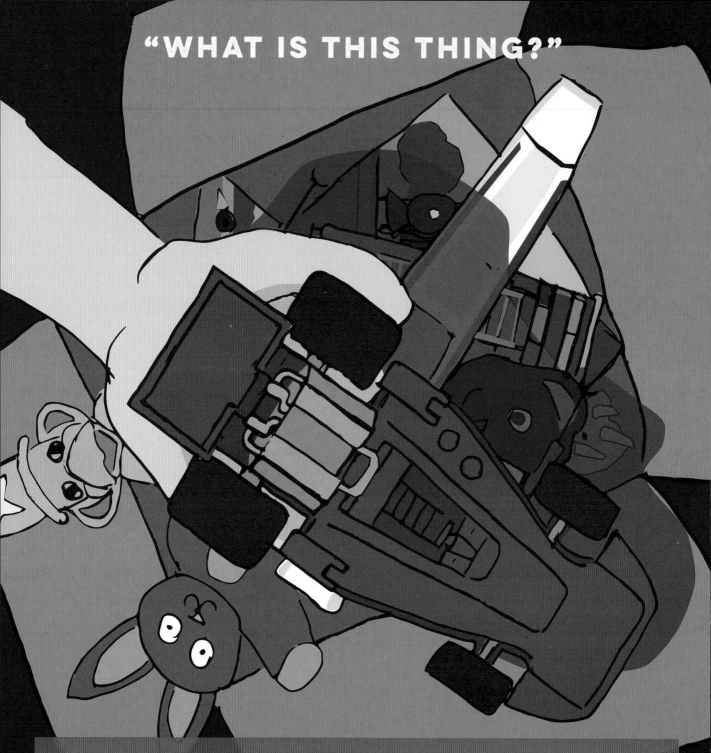

One May morning, Cooper was playing in his basement. He decided to look through some old boxes of toys to see if there was anything different to play with. He saw some dinosaurs, puzzles and space toys... then something caught his eye.

It looked like a toy race car of some type but Cooper had never seen anything like this before. He went upstairs to find his dad.

"Dad, what is this thing?" asked Cooper.

Dad said, "That, my boy, is A.J. Foyt's Gilmore Racing Coyote, which he drove to his fourth and final Indianapolis 500 victory... in miniature. There's an A.J. figure, van, trailer and mechanic down there too."

"Wait... I thought A.J. Foyt just owned a race team... and why does this car look so different than the ones we watch on TV?"

"No son, A.J. is one of the greatest race car drivers who has ever lived. After he stopped driving, he continued as a team owner. That toy was given to me by Grandpa Jamie after he took me to my first Indy 500 way back in 1977. I was only five-years-old, but I will never forget the day that I saw A.J. win his fourth Indy 500!

"Wow, 1977? They've been racing the Indy 500 that long?"

Dad replied, "Longer... much longer! The first Indianapolis 500 took place in 1911. The race took over six hours since the drivers only averaged about 75 miles per hour! And they were racing on bricks..."

"Over 6 Hours... On bricks... In 1911?!?" Cooper was amazed by what he was hearing.

"You are just full of questions today! Tell you what – why don't you go get your sister and I'll give you both a quick history of the Indy 500. There are so many great stories about the amazing drivers, cars, engineers and teams that have competed to win this wonderful race.

Once you learn more, you'll quickly see why people call the Indianapolis 500 'The Greatest Spectacle in Racing'!"

Cooper went to get his sister, Avery, while Dad grabbed some books, old photos and his laptop. Once they were all back on the couch, the story began...

THAT'S A LOT OF BRICKS!

Dad started by telling the kids about how the Indianapolis Motor Speedway was built. "It all started way back in 1905 when businessman Carl Fisher dreamed of creating a test track for car builders in Indiana. His dream became a reality when the Indianapolis Motor Speedway was completed in 1909.

Hot air balloons were the first to race at the track - not cars! During the first few short car races, the tar & asphalt pavement crumbled, so 3.2 million bricks were used to cover the track. This is is how the track got the nickname, 'The Brickyard'."

"3.2 million bricks? That's a lot of bricks!" said Cooper.

TRACK LAYOUT

The track was designed as a perfect rectangle with rounded corners. Four turns connect two long straightaways and two "short chutes" for a total track length of 2.5 miles. The track layout has remained unchanged since it was completed.

THE FIRST 500

On May 30, 1911, forty cars lined up five-wide to take the start of the first-ever "International 500 Mile Sweepstakes Race" (this was the original name for the Indy 500). Unlike today, cars didn't qualify for the race - they started in the order in which their entry form was received.

RIDING MECHANICS

Every car carried a driver and a riding mechanic - the mechanic's job was to oil the engine, check for tire wear and watch for competitors.

There was one exception - Ray Harroun competed by himself using a wonderful new driving aid - the rear-view mirror!

Drivers must complete 200 laps of the Indianapolis Motor Speedway to reach the 500-mile distance. Although he started from 32nd position, Ray Harroun passed many competitors to win the race by nearly two minutes over the second place car of Ralph Mulford. It took Ray's bright yellow Marmon Wasp 6 hours 42 minutes to complete the 500 miles!

"Wow... it doesn't even take that long to drive to Grandpa Jamie's house," said Avery.

"Well, they weren't driving much faster than we do on the expressway. It would have been amazing to have been at the first race! Cars weren't as common as they are today; to see over thirty of them racing would have been incredible!" said Dad.

THE "GOLDEN ERA"

Interest and popularity in the Indy 500 increased over the next few years, launching "The Golden Era" of the event.

The race attracted many European drivers and car companies like Peugeot, Mercedes, Fiat and Isotta.

They competed against cars from American car builders such as National, Stutz, Delage and Frontenac.

Riding Mechanics were required in 1912; race organizers thought it was safer than just having a driver in the car.

PEUGEOT

French car maker Peugeot was the first foreign car to win the Indy 500. They won in 1913 and 1916.

Howdy Wilcox won the 1919 Indy 500 in a Peugeot, but the big news was that qualification speeds exceeded 100 mph for the first time in history!

RALPH DEPALMA

Ralph DePalma was a tough competitor who had plenty of bad luck at the Speedway. In 1912, he led the first 194 laps and was ahead by 11 minutes only to lose after having engine troubles. He pushed his car across the finish line to complete the race!

Ralph won the 1915 Indy 500 for Mercedes, but lost again in 1921 when his engine broke while he was leading by two laps. Ralph led a total of 612 laps at Indianapolis - a record that stood until Al Unser Sr. broke it in 1987!

MILLER VS. DUESENBERG

"Many different types of cars tried to win the Indy 500 in the 1920's, but every race was won by either Miller or Duesenberg," Dad explained.

"Dues... en... berg?" Cooper tried saying. "You got it - they were a big American car builder back then."

Jimmy Murphy crossed the finish line first in his Duesenberg fitted with a Miller engine in 1922. This was the first year an engine designed by the legendary Harry Miller won at the Brickyard! Then, Harry focused on building entire racecars featuring his race engine.

LOUIS MEYER

Louis Meyer was the first driver to win three Indy 500s - all of them in cars powered by Miller engines. Louis won in 1928, 1933 and 1936.

In the early 1920's, Miller cars competed against Mercedes, Packard, Bugatti and racing versions of the Ford Model-T, but Duesenberg was Harry's main competition. Miller cars won four times between 1923 and 1929; Duesenberg won the other races.

TOMMY MILTON

In 1923, Tommy Milton became the first repeat winner of the Indy 500. His first win was in 1921 driving a Frontenac race car.

NO RELIEF

George Saunders was the first driver to win without the help of a relief driver in 1927. Relief drivers allowed the main driver to rest during long events.

THE MORE THINGS CHANGE...

"... the more they stay the same. At least that's how it was in the 1930's at the Indy 500," said Dad.

"Why's that, Dad?" asked Avery.

"The track owners created new rules to attract big car builders to race, but the new rules didn't prevent Henry Miller from winning just about every race in the 1930's!"

Former driver and World War I fighter pilot Eddie Rickenbacker became the new owner of the Indianapolis Motor Speedway in 1927.

He created a new set of rules to attract car builders like Chrysler, Buick, Hudson and Stutz to enter race cars in the Indy 500. Harry Miller also created new engines and cars to meet the new rules.

Harry's cars dominated with drivers such as Louis Schneider, Fred Frame and Bill Cummings behind the wheel! In 1930, Billy Arnold won after leading 198 out of the 200 laps - a record that still stands today!

Between 1936 and 1938, all of the original brick track surface was paved over with asphalt except for a section of the front straight.

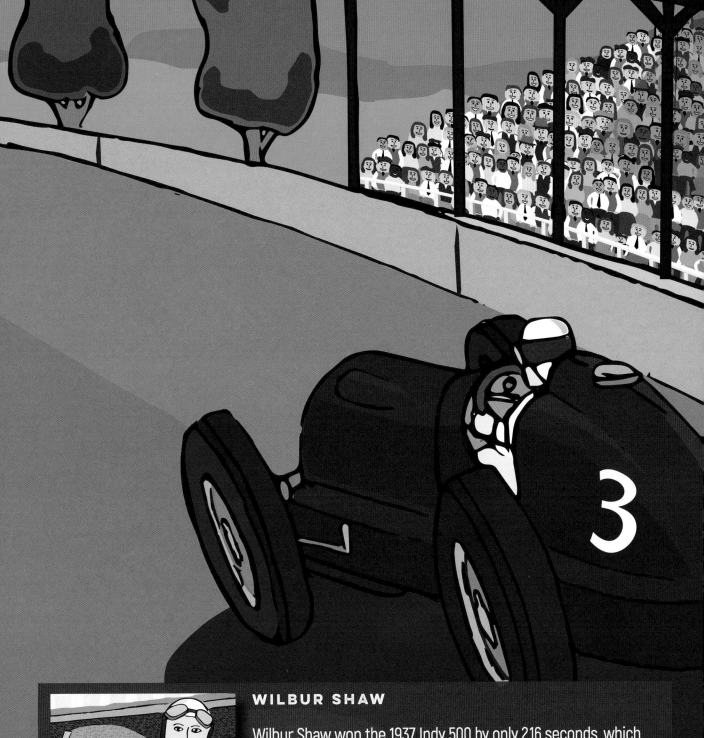

WILBUR SHAW

Wilbur Shaw won the 1937 Indy 500 by only 2.16 seconds, which was the closest margin of victory until 1982. Wilbur had a large lead but his car began to have issues with 20 laps to go - he was just barely able to hold onto the lead on the last lap!

Wilbur then became the first to win two races in a row in 1939 and 1940 driving a Maserati!

MILLER + "OFFY" = 39 VICTORIES

"For over 50 years, if a driver and team wanted a chance of winning the Indy 500, they used a car powered by one of Harry Miller's engines," Dad said. "It's amazing that the basic designs created by Harry won 39 times in 56 tries!"

"That's like a 70% win record!" said Avery.

"Yep - and as you'll learn a lot changed during these six decades, which makes this win record even more amazing!" Dad said.

BILL CUMMINGS
Miller-Miller 1934

RODGER WARD
Watson-Offy 1959

MILLER ENGINE

When Harry Miller's engines first appeared at Indianapolis in 1920, it started a legacy of winning that lasted until 1976. The Miller engines won a total of twelve times.

Harry went bankrupt in 1933 and one of his engine designers, Fred Offenhauser, purchased the designs for a new engine that Harry had originally built for boat racing.

"OFFY" ENGINE

Fred Offenhauser continued to develop Harry's new engine design. He beat a field full of Miller-engined cars to win his first Indy 500 in 1935. The engine was nicknamed "Offy" and from the late 1940's to early 1960's the "Offy" dominated the Indy 500, powering every winner for 18 years in a row.

BOBBY UNSER
Eagle-Offy 1968

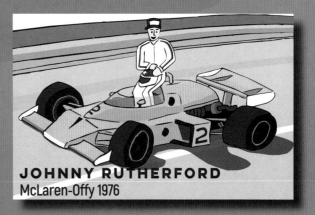

JOHNNY RUTHERFORD
McLaren-Offy 1976

VICTORIES IN FIVE DECADES!

In total, the "Offy" won the Indy 500 27 times. The last victory was in 1976 when Johnny Rutherford won for the second time at the Brickyard in a McLaren.

The original "Offy" engine had 250 hp, but thanks to ongoing development and turbocharging, the final version had over 1,000 hp!

THE HULMAN ERA

During World War II, the Indianapolis Motor Speedway stood still. By the time the war was over the track was in need of repair from lack of attention and the track was put up for sale. Three-time winner Wilbur Shaw helped find a buyer to keep the track and Indy 500 event alive. Soon, Indiana businessman Tony Hulman became the new owner of the Brickyard. The track has been owned by the Hulman family ever since.

TRACK IMPROVEMENTS

Tony worked quickly to fix the track for the race to resume in 1946. Areas of focus included building more grandstands, new garages and a scoring pylon.

Gasoline Alley: The garage area is known famously as "Gasoline Alley" - it is a favorite spot for fans to see cars up close!

Pagoda: The Speedway's unique Pagoda scoring tower behind the front straight has changed over the years! The wooden Pagoda building was repaired prior to the track reopening in 1946. A new, more modern structure was built in 1956. A completely new Pagoda was built prior to the 2000 Indy 500.

Paving over the bricks: In 1961, the last section of bricks was paved over except for a three-foot section of bricks at the Start-Finish line. This "yard of bricks" serves as a reminder to the track's great heritage.

MONTH OF MAY

For most motorsports events, all practice, qualifying and race activities are held within one weekend. Not the Indy 500!

For decades, the entire month of May was spent at The Speeday for rookie orientation, practice, two weekends of qualifying and then the race.

In recent times, the schedule has been reduced to two weeks. Since 2014, the Grand Prix of Indianapolis has been run on the Speedway's road course to kick off the Month of May!

"Carburetion Day" is the Friday before the Indy 500. It is the last day the cars are on track before the big race. Fans enjoy being able to see all the cars practice together and guess who has the strongest car for the race!

"OFFY MONSTERS"

Specialty race car builders worked to make their cars sleeker and lower from 1946 - 1964. These cars could be monsters to drive, but their "roadster" design was pretty simple - "Offy" engine up front, driver in the middle and a large fuel tank behind the driver.

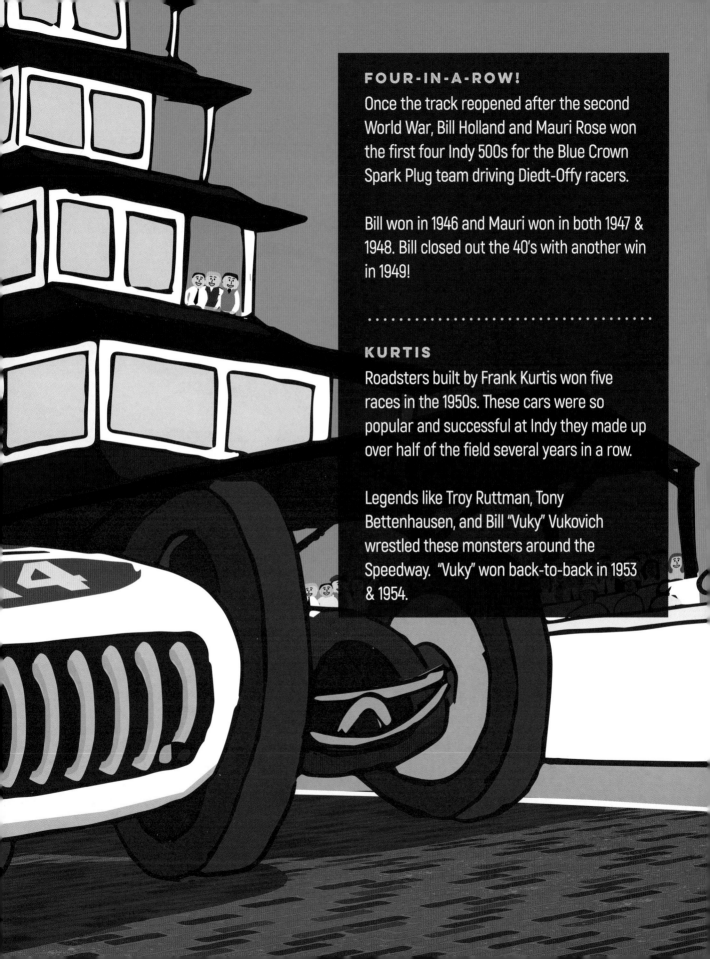

FOUR-IN-A-ROW!

Once the track reopened after the second World War, Bill Holland and Mauri Rose won the first four Indy 500s for the Blue Crown Spark Plug team driving Diedt-Offy racers.

Bill won in 1946 and Mauri won in both 1947 & 1948. Bill closed out the 40's with another win in 1949!

. . . .

KURTIS

Roadsters built by Frank Kurtis won five races in the 1950s. These cars were so popular and successful at Indy they made up over half of the field several years in a row.

Legends like Troy Ruttman, Tony Bettenhausen, and Bill "Vuky" Vukovich wrestled these monsters around the Speedway. "Vuky" won back-to-back in 1953 & 1954.

WORLD CHAMPIONSHIP OF DRIVERS

The Indy 500 was part of the Formula 1 World Championship from 1950 - 1960, however few Formula 1 teams and drivers participated in the race.

In 1952, Ferrari and Alberto Ascari made an appearance, but finished 31st after Alberto spun due to a broken wheel.

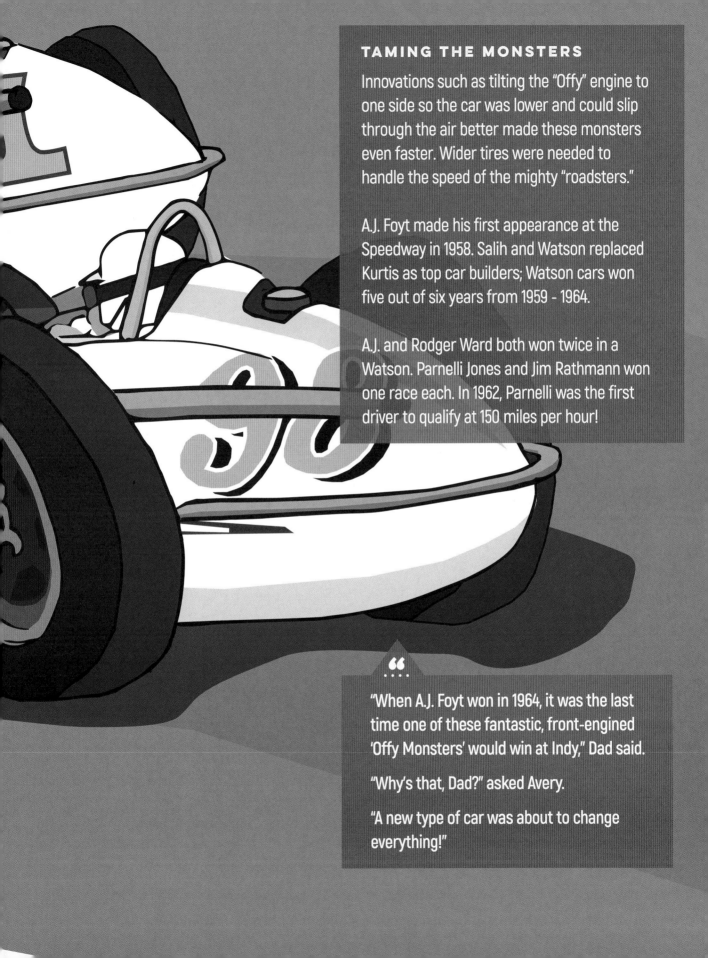

TAMING THE MONSTERS

Innovations such as tilting the "Offy" engine to one side so the car was lower and could slip through the air better made these monsters even faster. Wider tires were needed to handle the speed of the mighty "roadsters."

A.J. Foyt made his first appearance at the Speedway in 1958. Salih and Watson replaced Kurtis as top car builders; Watson cars won five out of six years from 1959 - 1964.

A.J. and Rodger Ward both won twice in a Watson. Parnelli Jones and Jim Rathmann won one race each. In 1962, Parnelli was the first driver to qualify at 150 miles per hour!

"

"When A.J. Foyt won in 1964, it was the last time one of these fantastic, front-engined 'Offy Monsters' would win at Indy," Dad said.

"Why's that, Dad?" asked Avery.

"A new type of car was about to change everything!"

THE BRITISH INVASION

"It started small. A single, spindly grand prix car arrived at The Brickyard in the early 60's. It didn't cause people too much concern, but it should have," Dad said.

"Why's that?" asked Avery.

"The engine was in the rear. While the car's tiny engine made it slower than the front-engined cars on the straights, it was much faster than them in the corners. Within a few years every car had its engine in the rear!"

" "

British car builders such as Cooper, Lotus and Lola pioneered rear-engined Indy cars using their Formula 1 experience. And, British Grand Prix drivers like Jim Clark, Graham Hill and Jackie Stewart, along with Australian Jack Brabham, took on the Americans at The Brickyard.

It was an exciting time at Indy! Jim won in his Lotus-Ford in 1965, and since then every Indy 500 has been won by a rear-engined car. The era of the "roadsters" was over!

COOPER-CLIMAX

THE AMERICAN RESPONSE

American race car builders were quick to respond, with "Offy"-powered rear-engined racecars from Vollstedt, Watson, Brawner, Halibrand & Gerhardt competing against the British cars.

Many "Old Guard" drivers had a difficult time switching from the "roadsters" to the rear-engined cars, but it didn't take long for A.J. Foyt to get to victory lane in 1967.

Driving legends Bobby Unser, Mario Andretti and Al Unser Sr. continued the string of Americans winning at Indy in the new era of rear-engined cars.

FEATURED ENGINES
FORD | FOYT | COSWORTH

Ford's appearance at Indianapolis in the 60's started an engine battle with "Offy."

Ford won the Indy 500 six times between 1965 and 1971. A.J.'s team took over the Ford engine program and renamed them "Foyt" in 1972. They scored one win in 1977.

Cosworth created an engine based on the Ford motor - it won ten races in a row from 1978 - 1987. Two more wins in 1995 & 1996 brings the total of Ford | Foyt | Cosworth wins to 19!

"Dad, why are those large metal pieces sitting behind the driver?" asked Avery.

"Now that engines were at the rear of the car, race car designers tried all sorts of new ways to use air to push the car onto the ground so it would go through turns faster," Dad said. "These metal pieces were the first wings used at Indy... but they were about to get much bigger!"

WINGS

"It all changed again in 1972. That's the first year wings were really allowed at the Speedway. Before then, the metal pieces were small and too close to the car, " Dad said.

"Did the wings help the cars go faster?" asked Avery.

"Did they ever! The cars went over 20 mph faster that year!
. . . .
"

A DIFFERENT KIND OF FLYING

These wings act just like airplane wings - only upside down. So, instead of helping lift the car up, the wings push it into the pavement. This helps the cars turn better and faster.

The impact was huge once larger "bolt on" wings were used. Bobby Unser qualified his Eagle-Offy at a speed of 195 mph - 17 mph faster than Peter Revson's wingless McLaren-Offy was able to reach the year before!

SOARING EAGLES

Indianapolis also caught the eye of racing legend Dan Gurney. He first drove at Indy in 1962; then he raced modified versions of his Eagle grand prix cars at the Brickyard starting in 1966.

Dan's All American Racers team was very innovative and constantly worked on new design ideas to find more speed. They were successful in winning the Indy 500 three times - in 1968, 1973 and 1975!

SPEED DEMONS

"Racecar designers continued to try different things to make the cars faster, " Dad explained. "They improved the wings but also learned new tricks... all with a goal of becoming the first to reach 200 mph at the Indianapolis Motor Speedway!"

CHAPARRAL

Texan Jim Hall was very involved in developing new ideas to increase speed - especially in turns. His Chaparral racer featured large tunnels beneath the car.

Air that flowed through these tunnels acted like a vacuum and sucked the car onto the track! Johnny Rutherford drove the Chaparral to win his third Indy 500 in 1980.

TOM SNEVA - FIRST TO 200 MPH

For the next few years, top drivers like Al Unser Sr., Mario Andretti, Tom Sneva, Johnny Rutherford, Gordon Johncock and A.J. Foyt chased the 200 mph barrier.

Tom was the first driver to ever qualify over 200 mph. After finishing second three times, Tom won the Indy 500 in 1983 by passing Al Sr. late in the race.

FASTEST EVER - ARIE LUYENDYK

Also known as "The Flying Dutchman," Arie Luyendyk won his first-ever Indy car race in big style by leading the last 32 laps of the 1990 Indy 500. In 1996, he drove the fastest single qualifying lap at Indy with a speed of 237.498 mph; his four-lap average was 236.986 mph.

Arie won again in 1997. He became the first person since A.J. Foyt to win Indy 500s driving race cars both with and without a turbo-charged engine.

THE "SPECIALS"

For many years, the word "special" was used to describe purpose-built Indy 500 race cars. But from time-to-time something truly unique turned up at The Brickyard - here are a few of the most inventive "specials" ever!

TURBINE CAR

One of the strangest cars ever appeared at The Brickyard in 1967. The car featured a helicopter jet engine placed next to the driver.

Parnelli Jones qualified 6th and quickly jumped into the lead, only to have a mechanical failure with three laps to go! Lotus designed a turbine car for 1968 - again the car nearly won but another issue forced the car out of the race.

SIX-WHEELER

In 1948, the first and only six-wheeled car appeared at the Indy 500. It was fast on the straights but slow in the turns. Billy DeVore drove the car to 12th place.

HURST FLOOR SHIFTER SPECIAL

This unique machine was built by stock car legend Smokey Yunick in 1964. The driver sat in a sidecar; it was very unsafe and thankfully it failed to qualify for the race.

CUMMINS DIESEL

Diesel engines use less fuel. The 1931 Clessie Cummins diesel powered Duesenberg was the first car ever to finish without refueling once during the race!

The 1952 Cummins Diesel "Special" got pole position - which means it started in first place. It would have won if the air inlet for the engine hadn't gotten clogged!

"BEAST"

In 1994, new rules were created to invite more car builders to race engines based on road cars in the Indy 500. Team Penske and their engine partner Ilmor-Mercedes created a brand-new, super-powerful secret engine instead! It qualified on pole position and won the race!

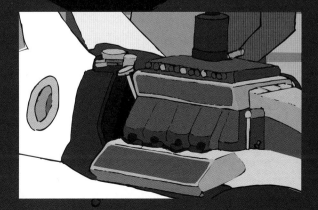

EMMO VS. "LITTLE AL"

"Indy 500 drivers race close together at very high speeds. They all want to win badly and they race hard against each other. Sometimes they push so hard they cause a wreck, or they make a mistake and crash themselves," Dad said.

"I bet they get pretty angry when that happens," said Cooper. Dad replied "Usually... but not always..."

"LITTLE AL'S" SPORTSMANSHIP LESSON

In 1989, Al Unser Jr. (aka "Little Al") and Emerson Fittipaldi were locked in a tight late-race battle when they made contact on lap 199, sending "Little Al" hard into the wall. In an impressive show of sportsmanship, Al Jr. applauded his rival and gave him a "thumbs up" for the great, hard racing as "Emmo" passed him on his way to victory!

Five years later, "Little Al" and Emerson were teammates at Team Penske and favored to win thanks to their "Beast" engine. "Emmo" was leading and ahead of "Little Al" by almost a full lap late in the race. "Emmo" knew if he could pass his teammate he would put him a lap down and he would most likely win. But, he pushed too hard and on lap 185 he spun and crashed, giving Al Jr. the win!

FEATURED ENGINE - CHEVY

Chevy entered the Indy 500 for the first time as an engine supplier in 1985. They won powering Rick Mears to his third Indy 500 win in 1988 - and then won six straight races!

The brand won again in 2002 and then stopped racing at Indy after 2005. They have won twice since rejoining competition in 2012; Chevy has won a total of nine Indy 500s so far!

LATE RACE RESTARTS

"The drama of the Indy 500 sometimes increases due to a late-race caution period caused by a crash," Dad said. "Then, when the green flag drops the long 500-mile race suddenly turns into a short sprint to the finish!"

1996 - LAZIER VS. JONES

Alessandro Zampedri, Davy Jones and Buddy Lazier were locked in a battle with only 10 laps to go. Scott Sharp's car spun and crashed, which brought out a yellow flag. Buddy took the green flag in the lead and won by holding off Davy for the last two laps!

1986 - RAHAL VS. COGAN VS. MEARS

A late-race caution caused by a crash closed the gap between the top three drivers. The race restarted with two laps to go; Kevin Cogan was in the lead followed by Bobby Rahal and Rick Mears.

Bobby got the jump on Kevin and took the lead into turn 1. Bobby kept the lead and won by only 1.4 seconds! He won again as a team owner in 2004 with Buddy Rice as his driver.

2012 - FRANCHITTI VS. SATO VS. DIXON

The race went green with only a few laps left in the race. Dario Franchitti traded the lead with Scott Dixon several times. Dario passed Scott on lap 199 and Takuma Sato also got by. On the last lap, Takuma dove to the inside to pass but spun, giving Dario the win!

THE FOUR-TIMER CLUB

"Winning the Indy 500 takes incredible skill, focus and luck for the driver and the team. Winning it once is amazing," Dad said. "think about what it would be like to win it four times!"

"Is that even possible?" asked Avery.

"It sure is, but only three men have accomplished this awesome feat. Seven other drivers have been able to get three wins," Dad said.

THREE-TIME WINNERS

Seven drivers have achieved the feat of winning the Indy 500 three times:

Helio Castroneves (2001, 2002, 2009), Dario Franchitti (2007, 2010, 2012), Louis Meyer (1928, 1933, 1936), Mauri Rose (1941, 1947, 1948) Johnny Rutherford (1974, 1976, 1980), Wilbur Shaw (1937, 1939, 1940), Bobby Unser (1968, 1975, 1981).

A.J. FOYT (AKA "SUPER TEX")

A.J. Foyt first competed at Indianapolis in 1958 and his last race as a driver was in 1992 - that's an incredible 35-straight Indy 500 starts!

A.J. first won in 1961. His victory in 1964 was the last time a front-engined car won at Indy. Then, "Super Tex" became the first driver to win in both front- and rear-engined cars by avoiding a large last-lap wreck in 1967. His final win came in 1977 driving his bright-orange #14 Coyote-Foyt racer.

A.J. reached victory lane for a fifth time as a team owner in 1999 when Kenny Brack drove another #14 for the win!

A.J. raced 12,272.5 miles at Indianapolis Motor Speedway - more than any other person - and led a lap in a record 13 events.

Add together his time as a driver and team owner and "Super Tex" has been a part of the Indy 500 for over half a century!

AL UNSER, SR. (AKA "BIG AL")

The Unser family holds a total of nine Indy 500 victories, and Al Unser Sr. stands as the leader scoring four wins in 27 starts and a record 644 laps led at the Brickyard. Al Sr. won back-to-back races in 1970 and 1971 driving the Johnny Lightning Team's P.J. Colt Ford; his third win came in 1978 driving a Lola-Cosworth.

Perhaps "Big Al's" most amazing victory came in 1987. After Team Penske driver Danny Ongais was injured in a practice accident, Al Sr. was asked to drive in his place.

The car was a replacement too - the team decided to race a car they knew could last the distance. The problem was, this older car was on display in a hotel lobby!

"Big Al" drove a steady race - he moved up the field as many faster competitors dropped out of the race. Roberto Guerrero stalled his car on his last pit stop, giving "Big Al" the lead with 17 laps to go. The veteran reserve driver brought the backup car home for the win!

RICK MEARS

This Californian known for off-road racing failed to qualify for his first Indy 500 in 1977. But, Roger Penske saw Rick Mears' potential and hired him to drive for his team.

The following year, Rick qualified on the front row. He took the lead with 18 laps to go to win the 1979 Indy 500. Rick had an easy win in 1984 when his two biggest competitors dropped out halfway through the race!

In 1988, Rick beat Penske teammates Danny Sullivan and Al Unser Jr. He became only the third driver to win four Indianapolis 500s when he won a late-race battle with Michael Andretti in 1991!

Rick also won a record six Indy 500 pole positions!

IN THE BLINK OF AN EYE

"Cooper, blink your eyes," said Dad. "How long do you think it took to blink?"

"Less than a second?" said Cooper "I was fast!"

"You are close," said Dad. "It was about a half a second. Can you believe that five times the Indy 500 winner crossed the finish line ahead of second place in less time than that?!?"

THE DUEL - 1982

The 1982 Indy 500 featured one of the best driving battles ever. An accident early in the race knocked out four top contenders and by lap 180 only Gordon Johncock and Rick Mears were the only cars on the lead lap. But, the on-track action was just heating up for these two legends!

Both cars needed a final pit stop for fuel. Rick took on a full fuel load and Gordon filled his tanks part-way. This strategy gave Gordon an 11-second lead, but his car was handling poorly. Rick's car was much faster and he was quickly catching Gordon!

With only three laps to go, the two drivers were only a few seconds apart. Rick gained more ground as the two weaved through lapped cars - the drivers were side-by-side as they took the white flag for the last lap!

The cars nearly touched entering Turn 1, which forced Rick to back-off. He caught Gordon and was on his tail going through the final turn. As the two drivers raced to the finish line, Rick swerved to make a pass but was one car-length short. Gordon won by only .16 seconds!

A BLUR OF YELLOW - 2014

A bad crash with nine laps to go brought out a red flag to stop on-track action so workers could fix damaged fencing. When the race restarted, fans saw a straight fight between the bright yellow racecars of Helio Castroneves and Ryan Hunter-Reay.

Helio took the lead with six laps to go, but Ryan wasn't about to give up! The two swapped positions twice before Ryan grabbed the lead with a difficult pass on the last lap. Helio caught up and tried to make a pass as they raced to the finish line, but Ryan held on for the win by only .060 seconds!

CLOSEST FINISH EVER - 1992

The closest victory in Indy 500 history came in 1992 when Al Unser Jr. held off a hard-charging Scott Goodyear. Michael Andretti dominated the race leading 160 laps, but with 12 laps to go his fuel pump failed and his car slowed on the track; causing a caution period.

The green flag waved with seven laps to go, and Al Jr. and Scott embarked on an epic battle to the finish. The two drivers were nose-to-tail as they sped around the track - "Little Al" somehow managed to keep Scott behind him.

Al Jr.'s car wiggled and slowed slightly in the last turn, which gave Scott a chance to try and pull off a slingshot pass as they raced to the finish line. Scott came up .043 seconds short!

SO CLOSE, YET SO FAR

"Imagine being in the lead on the last lap of your first-ever Indy 500. How would that feel?" Dad asked.

"Awesome!" both kids replied together.

"Now imagine you get passed within sight of the finish line," Dad said.

"That would be awful! " Avery said. "To race that far and be so close to winning... has that really happened?"

"Twice," Dad said. "And both times it happened to rookies."

THE LAST SECOND PASS - 2006

Marco Andretti looked set to win when the green flag dropped to restart race action with four laps to go. But, Team Penske driver Sam Hornish, Jr. was also hungry for a win and quickly climbed up to second place.

Sam caught up to Marco on lap 199 and tried to pass him for the lead in Turn 2. Marco defended the move which caused Sam to lose some ground.

Before long, Sam was back on Marco's tail as the two drove their final lap of the race. Sam set up the perfect slingshot pass coming out of Turn 4 and passed Marco within 400 feet of the finish line to win by .645 seconds!

Not only was it Sam's first and only Indy 500 victory, but it was the first time a driver ever made a pass on the last lap for a win.

ONE TURN AWAY - 2011

JR Hildebrand took over the lead with two laps left in the race after many other drivers had to pit for fuel. JR and his Panther Racing team had been saving fuel with the goal of making it all the way to the end of the race without having to make another pitstop.

On the very last turn, he ran high on the track as he tried to pass a lapped car and crashed into the wall. Dan Wheldon passed JR's broken car within a few hundred feet of the finish line to record his second win at Indianapolis!

AGAINST ALL ODDS

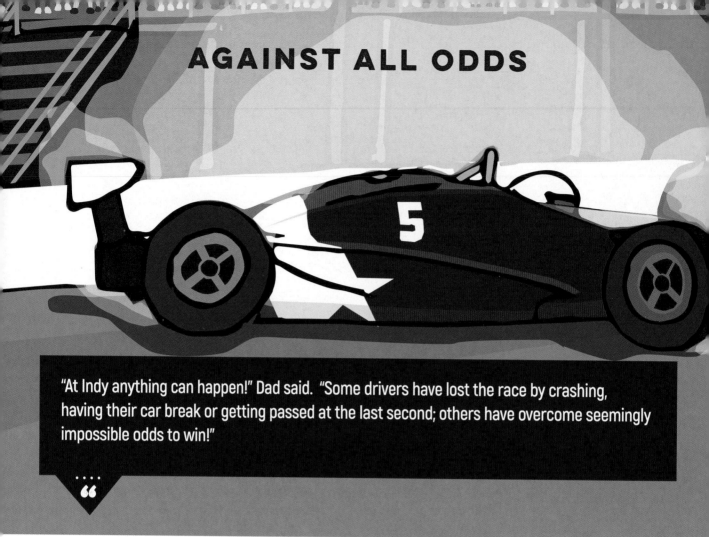

"At Indy anything can happen!" Dad said. "Some drivers have lost the race by crashing, having their car break or getting passed at the last second; others have overcome seemingly impossible odds to win!"

"

WIN FROM THE BACK - JUAN PABLO MONTOYA - 2015

The 99th Running of the Indy 500 saw the greatest come-from-behind victory in the history of the event!

It all started after Juan Pablo Montoya was hit from behind early in the race during a caution period. His rear-wing and bumper pod had to be replaced dropping him to 30th place.

While many drivers might have given up, Juan Pablo focused on working his way through the field to catch up to the leading cars.

A caution flag bunched up the cars and set the stage for a great battle between Juan Pablo, his Team Penske teammate Will Power and Chip Ganassi Racing driver Scott Dixon.

After the green flag dropped on lap 184, the lead changed four times until Juan Pablo slip-streamed by Will with four laps to go.

Despite Will's best effort, Juan Pablo held on for the win! This was Juan Pablo's second win - he also won in 2000 for Chip Ganassi Racing.

SPIN & WIN - DANNY SULLIVAN - 1985

The 1985 race featured one of the most amazing events in all of racing history. Danny Sullivan had caught up to Mario Andretti and was making a pass for the lead when he lost control and spun right in front of Mario in Turn 1.

Somehow Danny didn't hit anything during his spin. He sped off in pursuit of Mario and caught him 20 laps later. This time he made a clean pass for the lead and held on for his first and only Indy 500 win!

"THE CAPTAIN"

Many strong teams have competed at The Brickyard, and many teams have had great team owners, but none of them have been as successful as Roger Penske's team. Penske's cars first competed at the Indy 500 in 1969 and his team's first win came in 1972 when Mark Donohue drove a McLaren-Offy to victory.

Roger, who is also known as "The Captain," has won an astonishing 16 Indy 500 races - many of which have been featured in this book. Roger was also a race car driver - earning Sports Illustrated's Driver of the Year award in 1961!

UNDERDOGS

Teams with two or more cars usually have a better chance of winning at Indy. But, there have been several upsets over the years where an unexpected single-car underdog team has won the big race!

In 2013, KV Racing Technology won when Tony Kanaan made a late-race pass taking the lead from Ryan Hunter-Reay.

Many others have been covered in this book, such as: Bobby Rahal's win for Truesports in 1986, Emerson Fittipaldi gave Patrick Racing a win in 1989, Arie Luyendyk's huge upset victory for Doug Shierson Racing in 1990 and Dan Wheldon's 2011 win with Bryan Herta Autosport.

SPIDERMAN

Three-time winner Helio Castroneves brought a unique victory celebration to the Indy 500 when he won in 2001. After the traditional victory lap, Helio got out of his car on the front straight and climbed the track fence to celebrate with his Team Penske crew and the crowd.

PENSKE'S INDY WINS

1972 - Mark Donohue
1979 - Rick Mears
1981 - Bobby Unser
1984 - Rick Mears
1985 - Danny Sullivan
1987 - Al Unser Sr.
1988 - Rick Mears
1991 - Rick Mears
1993 - Emerson Fittipaldi
1994 - Al Unser Jr.
2001 - Helio Castroneves
2002 - Helio Castroneves
2003 - Gil de Ferran
2006 - Sam Hornish Jr.
2009 - Helio Castroneves
2015 - Juan Pablo Montoya

100TH RUNNING

The historic 100th Running of the Indianapolis 500 took place in 2016 and the finish was a real nail-biter!

Pole-winner James Hinchcliffe, Ryan Hunter-Reay and Josef Newgarden fought for the lead racing as hard as possible.

Rookie Alexander Rossi & his Andretti / Herta Autosport team used a fuel-saving strategy in the race so he would have fewer pitstops.

When front-running drivers Josef, Carlos Munoz and 2013 winner Tony Kanaan had to come in for a late-race splash of fuel, Alexander jumped up to first place!

Nearly out of fuel, Alexander slowed dramatically during the last two laps. He was able to just barely stay out front and win! It was very close though – he ran out of fuel on his victory lap!

FEATURED ENGINE - HONDA

Honda has been a top competitor at the Brickyard since 2003. Rahal-Letterman driver Buddy Rice gave the engine manufacturer their first win in 2004. Honda has won a total of 11 times so far powering cars from Target Chip Ganassi Racing, Bryan Herta Autosport, Andretti Autosport and Team Penske to victory!

"IT'S THE REAL THING!"

Avery and Cooper were amazed by the history of "The Greatest Spectacle in Racing." The kids wanted to learn more and luckily for them, Dad had the perfect solution to fuel their new interest... a family trip to the Indianapolis Motor Speedway Hall of Fame Museum!

They decided to plan their trip for the next weekend so they could also watch qualifying for the Indy 500. The kids were excited to visit the garages in Gasoline Alley to see the Indy cars up close. But first, they were meeting up with Grandpa Jamie at the museum.

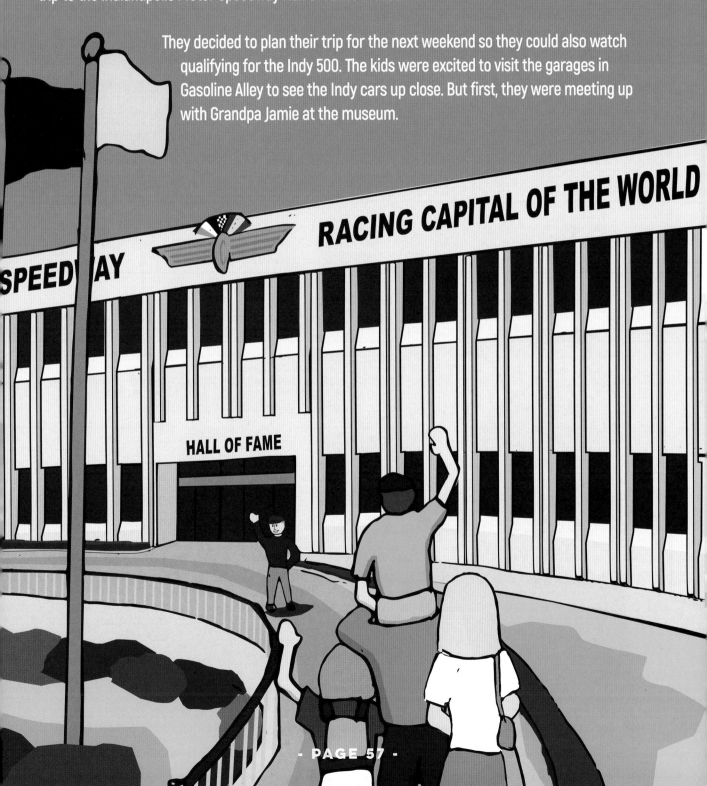

When they got into the museum the kids were amazed by how many cars they could see - they couldn't wait to check them all out!

Then they saw it - that familiar bright red-orange Coyote-Foyt race car was sitting on a stand in the museum under a skylight. "Look, Grandpa Jamie - it's the real thing!" Cooper shouted and ran up to the stand to take a closer look.

Avery followed Cooper over to the stand. The kids stood in awe of the beautiful race car. Dad and Grandpa Jamie smiled as they watched how excited the kids were to be in the museum, enjoying and learning about "The Spectacle."

Suddenly, Dad was the one staring in awe. "Is that who I think it is?" he asked Grandpa Jamie. "Sure is - it's 'Super Tex' himself!" Grandpa Jamie said with excitement.

Behind the very race car in which he won his fourth Indy 500, A.J. Foyt was talking to a reporter. Dad told the kids the news; Avery quickly unzipped her backpack and pulled out the old toy racecar.

"Think he'd sign it?" Avery asked. "Maybe... but let's not interrupt him," Dad said. "He seems busy."

But as Dad completed his sentence he looked up and saw A.J. walking around the Coyote-Foyt stand towards them. Avery lifted up the old toy and Cooper waved his arm to get A.J.'s attention.

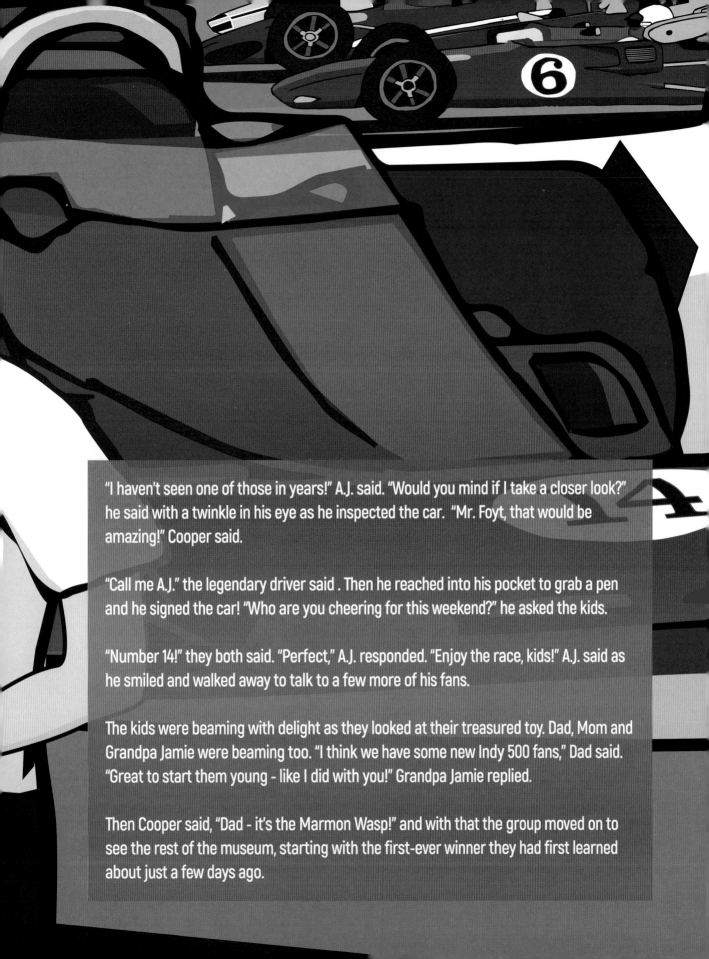

"I haven't seen one of those in years!" A.J. said. "Would you mind if I take a closer look?" he said with a twinkle in his eye as he inspected the car. "Mr. Foyt, that would be amazing!" Cooper said.

"Call me A.J." the legendary driver said . Then he reached into his pocket to grab a pen and he signed the car! "Who are you cheering for this weekend?" he asked the kids.

"Number 14!" they both said. "Perfect," A.J. responded. "Enjoy the race, kids!" A.J. said as he smiled and walked away to talk to a few more of his fans.

The kids were beaming with delight as they looked at their treasured toy. Dad, Mom and Grandpa Jamie were beaming too. "I think we have some new Indy 500 fans," Dad said. "Great to start them young - like I did with you!" Grandpa Jamie replied.

Then Cooper said, "Dad - it's the Marmon Wasp!" and with that the group moved on to see the rest of the museum, starting with the first-ever winner they had first learned about just a few days ago.

TRADITIONS & FUN FACTS

Sure, the racing is spectacular at Indy, but the event is truly special thanks to the traditions that create a unique atmosphere. Attend the race for yourself and you can't help but get caught up in the excitement!

THE SOUNDS

In 1946, Tom Carnegie became the track PA announcer - a position he held until 2006. Carnegie's signature way of building up anticipation during qualifying sessions and announcing "And it's a new... track... record!" delighted fans. The song "Back Home in Indiana" was first sung prior to the race in 1946; actor Jim Nabors sang this fan favorite many times until 2014.

VICTORY CELEBRATION

Louis Meyer was the first to drink milk in victory lane in 1936. Milk has been the victory lane drink of choice since 1956.

The Borg-Warner trophy was introduced in 1936. A small sculpture that looks like the winning driver is added to the trophy after each race.

The famed tradition of the Indy 500 winner kissing the start-finish line bricks was introduced by stock car driver Dale Jarrett after he won the 1996 Brickyard 400 NASCAR race.

SPEED CHART

Indy 500 racers have gotten faster over the years, but the top speed was recorded over 20 years ago! All speeds are from four-lap pole-position qualifying unless otherwise noted.

1911 - Ray Harroun - Marmon Wasp - 74.60 mph

1962 - Parnelli Jones - Watson-Offy - 150.37 r

75 mph (race average)   100 mph (1-lap qualifying)   125 mph (10-lap qualifying)   150 mph

1919 - Rene Thomas - Ballot - 104.78 mph   1938 - Floyd Roberts - Wetteroth-Miller - 125.68 mph

NOT JUST FOR THE BOYS...

Nine different women have qualified and raced in the Indy 500; here are four leading ladies:

Janet Guthrie was the first woman to qualify for the Indy 500 in 1977. She competed in three Indy 500s with a best finish of 9th.

Lyn St. James's first Indy 500 was 1992. She competed seven times and qualified as high as sixth; her best finish was 11th place.

Sarah Fisher was both a driver and team owner. She competed nine times as a driver with a top finish of 17th place.

Danica Patrick qualified as high as 3rd in seven starts and scored six top-ten finishes. In 2005, she became the first woman to ever lead laps in the Indy 500.

TIRE CHANGES

Did you notice how tires have changed in this book? At first, tires were very tall and narrow (4 in. wide) but over the years they've become shorter and wider. Modern Firestone race tires are 10 in. wide in front and 14 in. wide in back.

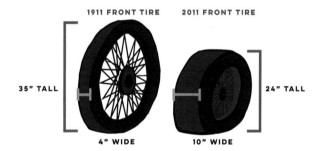

1911 FRONT TIRE   2011 FRONT TIRE

35" TALL   24" TALL

4" WIDE   10" WIDE

When cars became rear-engined, rear tires started getting wider. More importantly, tires switched from being grooved road tires to smooth "slicks" made from sticky rubber that helps grip the track!

1978 - Tom Sneva - Penske-Cosworth - 202.16 mph

1996 - Arie Luyendyk - Reynard-Ford Cosworth - 236.98 mph

175 mph   200 mph   220 mph   236 mph

1971 - Peter Revson - McLaren-Offy - 179.69 mph   1989 - Rick Mears - Penske-Chevrolet Indy - 223.86 mph

ENJOY OTHER TITLES FROM APEX LEGENDS!

If you enjoyed this book and want to share more stories about racing with your kids, go to ApexLegends.com to learn more about our other titles. New projects are already underway for future release!

THE LONGEST DAY - A CHILDHOOD RACE ADVENTURE

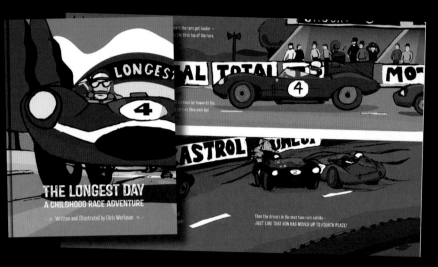

Read about how Grandpa Jamie fell in love with racing as a young boy!

In "The Longest Day - A Childhood Race Adventure," Jamison (aka Jamie) and his father travel to the grueling 24 Hours of Le Mans together and have a great adventure!

As the race action unfolds, the pair bond as they enjoy the sights, sounds and atmosphere of Le Mans and cheer for their favorite team.

JOSEF, THE INDY CAR DRIVER

"When it comes to fast reads, 'Josef, the Indy Car Driver' deserves a spot on any young racing fan's podium--or bookshelf." - AutoWeek

Apex Legends and Verizon IndyCar Series star Josef Newgarden have teamed up to create a unique racing-themed children's picture book unlike any other. "Josef, The Indy Car Driver" mixes Indy car racing education with entertaining on-track action that is sure to please budding race fans and their parents!

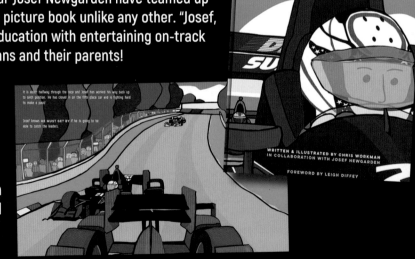

Set at iconic Road America, the content is designed to provide an authentic glimpse into the world of Indy car through Josef's eyes. While this book is certainly geared to appeal to core race fans, the underlying "chase your dreams" theme offered through Josef's true story serves as inspiration to all kids that anything is possible.

Sign up for The Inside Line enewsletter at ApexLegends.com or follow Apex Legend's social media for new product updates, special offers and more!

STAY CONNECTED   f APEX LEGENDS   🐦 @APEX LEGENDS   📷 APEX LEGENDS